THE
SLAVE
ROUTE

Old Barbary slave port, Bizerte, Tunisia, Africa

THE
SLAVE
ROUTE

From Africa
to America

HARRY
HOLCROFT

To Sarah

First published in Great Britain in 2003 by
ANTIQUE COLLECTORS' CLUB
Sandy Lane, Old Martlesham
Woodbridge, Suffolk
IP12 4SD

Designed by Bet Ayer

A CIP catalogue record for this book is available
from the British Library.

ISBN 1 85149 456 1

Set in Venetian
Printed in Spain

CONTENTS

FOREWORD

This book is the third in the trilogy — *The Silk Route*, *The Spice Route* and *The Slave Route*. Having travelled both the Silk and Spice Routes, it was natural to continue with Man's incessant quest of wealth and so travel the Slave Routes.

As an artist my reason for travelling is always visual. But, as with the Silk and Spice Routes, I recorded my thoughts and circumstances, as I perceived, in countries I visited. Slavery was, and is, worldwide. It has been central to human existence and extends far beyond the imagination. In this book, however, I have concentrated only on slavery between Europe, Africa and the Americas. The subject is too vast for only one book.

All pictures in this book are now in the hands of private collectors.
I thank them for their patronage and continued support.

The book is set out geographically rather than chronologically,
therefore diary dates and events do not necessarily follow in sequence.
Narratives in italics are extracts taken directly from my diaries.

INTRODUCTION

PAGAN, BURMA (FROM *THE SPICE ROUTE*)
Sunday 28 February 1999

It is sunset. I gaze to the West across the Irrawaddy River. Temple upon temple shimmer throughout the haze, and I wonder at their magnificence, and think of Coleridge.

'In Xanadu did Kublai Khan a Stately Pleasure dome decree' ... Decree?

The vast monuments of antiquity throughout the world were built by decree — but constructed by slaves.

Silk and spice may have caused the greatest trading routes in mankind's history, but slaves have been the oldest and most long-lasting bedrock of human wealth and development.

SLAVERY

Of all institutions, common to all societies throughout human history, slavery is the only constant. It would not be wildly inaccurate to suggest that well over 90% of all humanity has been subjected to slavery in one form or another.

Prehistoric graves in Lower Egypt indicate that a Libyan people living before 10,000BC had enslaved the indigenous 'Bushmen' or 'Hottentots'.

In the West in recent history (i.e. the last 2000 years), when the Roman Empire collapsed, ancient institutions did so with it – as did families, gods, and traditions. The only thing that survived – as a coherent organisation amidst the chaos – was slavery.

Today 'Slave Trains' (I use the word 'train' in the modern mechanical sense) leave Khartoum for Southern Sudan purely for slave trading. International aid agencies pay these traders, in an attempt to free those enslaved. All this does is inflate prices, so the trade continues ever stronger.

In Mauritania in West Africa slavery was only abolished in 1980. It is estimated that up to 100,000 black Africans in this country are still enslaved today by their Moorish

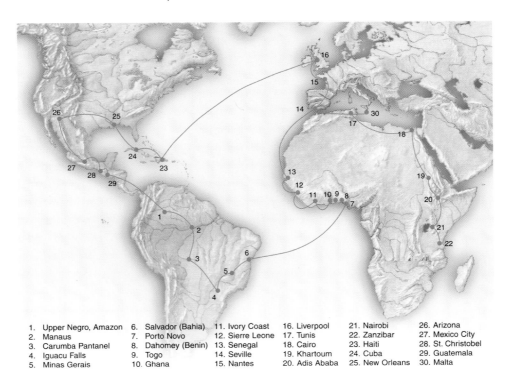

1. Upper Negro, Amazon	6. Salvador (Bahia)	11. Ivory Coast
2. Manaus	7. Porto Novo	12. Sierre Leone
3. Carumba Pantanel	8. Dahomey (Benin)	13. Senegal
4. Iguacu Falls	9. Togo	14. Seville
5. Minas Gerais	10. Ghana	15. Nantes

16. Liverpool	21. Nairobi	26. Arizona
17. Tunis	22. Zanzibar	27. Mexico City
18. Cairo	23. Haiti	28. St. Christobel
19. Khartoum	24. Cuba	29. Guatemala
20. Adis Ababa	25. New Orleans	30. Malta

The slave routes I followed.

overlords. In Cote d'Ivoire the UN estimates that over 200,000 slave children work the cocoa plantations.

(Think next time you eat that bar of chocolate!)

From Cote d'Ivoire along the West African Coast to Nigeria — what was known as the Slave Coast — over 100,000 slave children are traded every year — even today.

No less harrowing is the use of child soldiers. In the very recent civil wars of Sierra Leone, Liberia and Cote d'Ivoire, virtually whole populations of rural children were drafted as child soldiers.

In one form or another, the institution has been the basis of human progression. Slaves built the first agricultural systems in Mesopotamia (the Fertile Crescent), allowing the rise of the first civilisation in 10,000BC. In China, around the same time, slaves built the vast hydraulic systems of the Yangtse and Yellow Rivers, allowing the rise of civilisation in the East.

Slaves built the Egyptian pyramids, as they did the Mayan and Aztec pyramids in the Americas. The Golden Years of Greece and Rome were the result of slavery. Slaves built the Parthenon.

At the height of the Roman Republic there were over two million slaves in Italy alone — the majority of the population! The whole Empire required a constant supply of half a million a year.

India's history is one of slavery. The 'caste' system inherent to Hinduism is a convenient means of subjugating people to specific roles in society — slavery in all but name.

In China the male population confined the female population to slavery through the process of 'footbinding'. The list goes on.

Today through China, India, Africa, the Middle East, Eurasia, the Americas and Indonesia — through varying degrees of indentured labour— slavery continues to under-pin our lives, and what we consume.

SLAVERY AND LAW – THE WEST – CHRISTIANITY

The Greeks were the first – as with most things – to start questioning slavery. Before them, the condition of slavery was assumed as coming from, and continuing to, the eternal. Throughout the world it was accepted as part of the human condition.

Aristotle stated unequivocally that humanity was divided into two: Masters and Slaves. 'Those who have the right to command and those who are born to obey'.

This, to the Athenians, came to mean that anyone who was not Greek could be captured and enslaved – and even should be. The same argument was used between Christians and Moslems and Europeans and Africans. Plato went further, arguing that the Slave should be likened to the Body, the Master to the Soul.

It was Rome, however, that first actually started codifying laws concerning slaves. Cicero and Seneca both

started the concept of restricting the rights of the master, specifically over life and death.

But, even during this time, when the Man we call Jesus Christ was walking in Jerusalem, He never once mentioned slavery, which gave credence to the belief that slaves were beyond divine consideration and this is specifically addressed in both Matthew and the Acts of the Apostles. St. Paul went further: 'Serve your master with fear and trembling', so actually condoning slavery. Ultimately it was argued that Christ came not to change social conditions, but to change minds: 'Non venit mutate conditiones sed mentes'.

Even during the later Christian era, St. Augustine accepted it unconditionally as the result of original sin: 'Slavery could not exist without the Will of God – who knows no injustice'.

In 1525 Martin Luther, the catalyst of the Reformation, rejected pleas for slave emancipation. He argued that the man Jesus Christ may have died to set Man free, but the Earthly Kingdom could only survive if some men were free and some were slaves.

It was not until the Atlantic Slave Trade had reached its zenith in the 1800s that the Abolitionists started using other sources to denounce it.

SLAVERY AND LAW – THE EAST – ISLAM

The most interesting fact for me about the African Slave Trade is this:

Islam accepted slavery, as did Christianity, as an unquestionable part of human organisation. Mohammet took over the system without question: although Sharia (Islamic Law) developed a more benign approach than that practised by Christianity.

However, Christian Europe transported 20 million Africans from West Africa to the Americas as slaves. Today they exist as thriving black communities – 400 million of them – admittedly, in many cases, in deprived circumstances, but far better than their brothers who remain in Africa.

Possibly 30 million were transported by Islam to the Middle East, India and South East Asia, from East Africa. Where are they?

They were not allowed to breed ... they were all castrated.

Sailing Boat, Irrawaddy, Burma

SLAVERY – WHY?

As I write, the United States of America is invading Iraq. Why? Why war? Why slavery? They both manifest all that is darkest in humanity.

Boswell writing on war in 1777: 'War is followed by no general good whatever. The power, glory, wealth of a very few may be enlarged. But the people in general upon both sides, after all the suffering is passed, pursue their ordinary occupations, with no difference from their former state'.

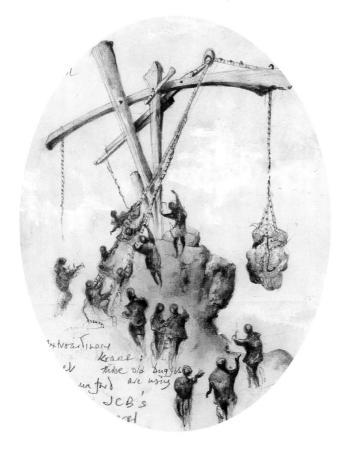

The evil of war is, as the French say, a 'pure perte' – a loss without any advantage. And slavery? As we grow we begin to perceive a flow of human conduct, which no amount of philosophical university education could ever influence.

We come face to face with Freud and his misgivings with regard to the underlying irresponsibility and irrationality of human nature and the propensity to mutual destruction. What Christianity has termed 'Original Sin'. The subjugation of one people over another: so war and slavery.

Liverpool, waterfront. A visual example of the wealth generated by slavery

EUROPE

Slavery is normality and has been world wide throughout Man's history.
The trade between West Africa and the Americas was driven by the Europeans, and in
particular by the English, although it had been started by the Portuguese.

Of course an iniquity but...

'Every Age has its own social context, its own climate, and takes it for granted.
To neglect this; to use terms like 'rational', 'superstitious', 'progressive',
'reactionary' as if only that which was traditional and obeyed OUR rules of reason,
is worse than wrong. It is vulgar.' *Hugh Trevor-Roper*

THE PORTUGUESE ADVANTAGE

There were a number of reasons why Portugal was so far ahead of England, France and Spain, in both exploitation and development of the Slave and Spice Routes during the 1400s. Her people, forced, like the English, to the margins of Europe, could only look seaward. Castile (Spain) was turned in on itself, always on the brink of Civil War. England was fighting the French in the early 1400s (Agincourt) and, in the second half of the century, was rattled by the conflicts of Henry II's children, Richard the Lionheart and King John.

Portugal, on the other hand, was economically and politically stable. There was a strong 'middle-merchant' class, the nobility having been destroyed in previous civil wars. Maritime activity and trading were part of the Portuguese psyche. They had encouraged the Jews and the Genoese, and had a healthy respect for both maps and the magnetic compass.

They were, historically, the geographical 'middleman' between Northern Europe and the Mediterranean. They had developed the lateral-rigged caravel. This was a modification of the Moorish vessels which had long been sailing off the North and West African Coast. The caravel's advantage was that it could sail closer to the wind than conventional craft, and hence move further faster.

Politically, Portugal also had the backing of the Papacy. Pope Nicholas V (a German) witnessed the fall of Constantinople to the Turks and the switch of trade from East to West – and so he actively encouraged Portuguese endeavours. Calixtus, his successor (the first of the Borgia Popes), made a solemn vow to recover Constantinople and

Seville. Centre of the European slave trade in 1400. The Cathedral.

gave Portugal 'Carte Blanche' by 'the Order of Christ' for exploration and trade to find the Indies. This was a direct result of Islamic control of the Spice Route throughout the Levant – strategically vital to Europe.

Finally there was the fabled 'King of the East', Prester John (Priest King John), and more importantly the power of a Christian Empire in Ethiopia (Coptic), to encircle the Islamic threat.

And also by 1480 the Portuguese had a monopoly of 'Trade' on the West African Coast. She was up and running alone, the primary reason to discover the Indies, via Africa.

INITIAL TRADING

With no competition, trade along the West African coast expanded. Pepper – known as Guinea Grain – was natural to what is present-day Senegal, Gambia and Sierra Leone (which became known as 'the Grain Coast'). Ivory – the Ivory Coast – and Gold – the Gold Coast – were other commodities that followed. The Moors had first started trading African slaves in Cadiz and Lisbon around 1250. It was due to this that the Portuguese subsequently began to regard the 'African' as another commodity.

The capture of the Canary Islands and Madeira in 1450 resulted in the first sugar plantations using West African slaves. This again was the result of the Islamic threat in the Levant to the sugar plantations of Venice in Crete, Cyprus, Sicily and Palestine.

So began one of history's most tragic associations: slaves and sugar. The climate of the Canaries was erratic and so sugar production was more suitable for the creation of rum which, in turn, became a commodity to equal pepper, gold, ivory and slaves.

EXPANSION

Expansion continued. In 1481 the first European structure on the African continent was built at Elmira (in present-day Ghana) – a basic but strong stone fort.

Originally built for safety, these structures provided storage and enabled a ship to make a quick turn-around. More were built, and became stepping stones along the West Coast of Africa – to establish the route to the Indies. Bartolomeu Diaz rounded the Cape in 1487.

So, before Columbus even set off to discover the Indies (i.e. the Americas), Portugal was manipulating huge empires far inland up the rivers of present-day Gambia, Senegal, Nigeria and the Congo. A flourishing trade in slaves had been established, but the commodity was not unusual.

By the 1540s Vasco da Gama was discovering vast and beautiful cities, flourishing on slavery, on the East African coast – Malindi, Mombasa, Mozambique, Madagascar.

The Portuguese merely, and effectively, intruded on an already established commercial network. Slavery had been central to it – centuries before they arrived. The Genoese, the Florentines (Medicis) all became involved, giving financial impetus to the eventual shipping of slaves to America.

Cape Coast, Ghana

DEVELOPMENT OF THE TRADE

THE RENAISSANCE

Renaissance translated means 'rebirth' or 'renewal'. Scholars will argue about dates, but I shall take the artist Giotto (painting in 1350) as its beginning and the completion of the Cistine Chapel by Michelangelo (around 1540) as its climax.

This is when slavery got its papal justification – or, in more modern terms, its adrenalin injection. 'Rebirth' took the arts and intellectual thoughts in Europe back to Greek and Roman antiquity, so continuing the acceptance of slavery as a natural human condition. Renaissance painters from Carpaccio to Tintoretto incorporated slaves in many of their paintings.

As such, it was during the Renaissance, and because of it, that the entire history of the Atlantic Slave Trade was set.

Far from being humanitarian, the Renaissance fostered the resignation of stoics, and a greater sum of intolerance!

Sidi Bin Said, Tunisia

THE TRIANGLE

A triangle of trade developed – one side, Europe to Africa; a second side, Africa to the Americas (the 'Middle Passage'); and a third side, the Americas back to Europe. The driving commodity? Obviously the slaves.

EUROPE TO AFRICA

For the purchase of slaves various commodities were shipped from Europe to Africa. The most important of these was cloth.

In the 1600s one piece of cloth large enough to cover the human body was equal to one slave. So not only was cloth imported from the Manchester Textile Mills (the 'Satanic Mills' of Blake), but silks from India and China as well, via the Dutch and the Portuguese.

After cloth it was metals. Africa, as we shall see, had a long history of iron smelting, which had caused total deforestation in large areas, for the charcoal. Iron bars and copper sheets were therefore highly prized. Iron came from Sweden, and Staffordshire – as well as the classic iron cauldrons, used by the cannibals for cooking missionaries (made, incidentally by one of my ancestors – the foundries of Thomas Holcroft!).

Then came shells – cowries. The word derives from the Hindu 'Kauri'. It was adopted by most of the Indian sub-continent, and also in Venice and the Mali Empire. 1 Slave = 6,000 Cowries in 1580. 1 Slave = 16,000 Cowries by 1780.

In Ouidah (Benin), between 1700 and 1800, 25 million pounds in weight of cowry shells were imported.

Cowries were an international currency, the same as paper money. An individual cowry had limited value – but was attractive to look at and handle, hard to break and neither faded nor wore. Cowries are impossible to counterfeit, hard to hoard and can be put to no other use.

Then alcohol. Despite indigenous alcohol from palm (wine), honey (mead), millet (beer), imported Madeira, Port and Muscadet became the early favourites.

By 1700 the distilling process had been invented by the Benedictine monks. Spirits became the great trade commodity. French Brandy and Brazilian Cane Brandy (1 barrel = 10-20 slaves).

And then rum. The effect was dreadful. African kings/chiefs would get drunk and then decide in the middle of the night to organise a raiding party for more slaves (to get more rum) – a dreadful vicious circle. By 1800 rum was the biggest export of the Americas and, along with gin, the biggest of the barter commodities.

And then finally tobacco, glass beads, crystal, coral and amber. Horses were also traded (1 horse = 25 slaves). As a unit of account they were amazingly attractive, but their disadvantage was they were cumbersome to transport.

However, the most consequential export was weapons. The Birmingham and London gunmakers had a field day, exporting around 300,000 pieces a year. Compare it to the arms industry today.

In 1500 1 gun = 1 slave. As a result, the Ashanti and Dahomey kingdoms developed an immense power base – out of the barrel of a gun – and became the most effective source of slaves, and fermented internal tribal conflicts.

FROM THE AMERICAS TO EUROPE

After 'The Middle Passage' (which we shall come to later), the slaving ships delivered their slave cargo to the Americas and returned to Europe.

They were laden with gold and gemstones for Portugal, Spain, England, France and Northern Europe, and also with cotton from the great cotton fields of Louisiana. However, the biggest export of all was sugar. Look at the portraits of the 1700s and 1800s by Gainsborough, Reynolds, Lawrence or Thompson and you see the plump rosy-cheeked females who became addicted to the stuff.

What has been historically termed 'the saccharin soul' of Britain's Golden Age was entirely dependent on sugar. Similarly, look at the females in the pictures of France: Boucher and Fragonard. Wonderful!

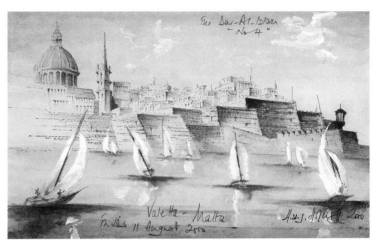

Valetta, Malta

Fort Angelo, Malta

LIVERPOOL AND LONDON

LIVERPOOL I

By the 1800s Britain dominated the slave trade. In 1780 the Prime Minister, William Pitt, stated in Parliament that four-fifths of all English trade was slavery. Half of the world's slave trade was conducted by the supposedly 'freedom loving and modern' British. This may, perhaps, give an indication of 'double standards' and the absurdity of political correctness.

Liverpool was the heart, although Nantes, in France, was a close second. Both had that sign of prosperity that never deceives – namely, big new buildings.

Such was the wealth of Nantes, for example, that the slave merchants sent their silk shirts to Haiti to be washed! Caribbean water supposedly made them whiter than French water. (Ludicrous though it may be, the French planters in Haiti were sending their shirts back to Paris, out of sheer extravagance!)

On the back of all this, London became the heart of the universe. Carlyle, the great commentator of the period, compared it to Babylon or Babel, with the added feeling that it had become an emblem of all that is darkest and extreme within existence itself.

Was this the heart of Empire or Conrad's *Heart of Darkness*, comparable now to all the West perceives as African darkness and the poverty and violence that goes with it? Trade became hysterical – fortunes and abject poverty lived side by side.

Lloyds, the coffee houses, the Guilds and the financial institutions went out of control – as they do today. And the 'Bubble' burst... as it always does.

This was the 'South Sea Bubble' of our schooldays. Incorrectly, our attention was drawn to the South Seas of India and Indonesia. What actually was at the heart of it was the slave trade.

LONDON

London became the equivalent of Rome and Egypt in their time. By 1850 it was the capital of the world. (Oddly, most of its population was enslaved to it.)

Today the remains of the vast cathedrals to Mammon – Canary Wharf and the Docklands, together with Liverpool's waterfront and the Bristol docks – are all the outward expression of slavery, as are the mammoth mansions of the North, designed to Neo-gothic excess – all built on the backs of slaves.

Liverpool, waterfront. A visual example of the wealth generated by slavery

Liverpool
RACISM I
8 February 2003

*T*o compare Liverpool with Venice is of course absurd – but there is a similarity – so I shall!

Both cities were born of water and trade. Both produced wealth, architecture, arts and grandiose extravagance. (The Doge's Palace in Venice compares to Castle Howard – although in Yorkshire – built on trade via Liverpool).

Where they diverge is the area of racial integration, because of British innate liberalism.

The Venetians were appallingly racist. Jewish and other ethnic groups hardly exist, in comparison to Liverpool.

Liverpool has the oldest and biggest Chinatown in Europe, as well as a direct African population: indentured labour. It also involved Indians, Greeks, Arabians, Vietnamese and, in the 20th century, Afro-West Indians. This obviously led to tension, expressed in the Toxteth Riots of 1983.

But do you see many black faces in Venice? I have not!

Which is more racist? – And this is during a period of alarm over asylum seekers.

LIVERPOOL II

With wealth came architectural and artistic splendour. With the exception of London, Liverpool has more listed buildings than any other city in the British Isles. Music and galleries abounded, and still do today (Liverpool being the cradle of modern popular 20th century music and the up and coming cultural centre of Europe).

The connection with slavery is everywhere. Street names: Gorée Wharf (from Senegal), Jamaica Street, and Tavleton and Cunliffe Streets named after Mayors of Liverpool who derived their position and wealth from owning slave ships. Cunliffe dispatched fifty-two slaving voyages during his lifetime. Not least 62 Rodney Street, home of William Ewart Gladstone, the great Liberal Prime Minister whose fortune was built on slavery.

And the Great British houses: Harewood, Blenheim, Castle Howard, and the works of Vanbrugh, the Adam brothers, Capability Brown, and Chippendale – from the wealth created by slavery.

The Banks
In 1826 Thomas Leyland formed Leyland Bank, which became the Midland Bank in 1908, now HSBC – based on slavery. In 1883 Arthur Heywood formed the Bank of Liverpool, which became Barclays Bank – based on slavery.

Industry
The Liverpool Manchester Railway and Ship Canal – financed by slavery. The slate quarries of North Wales, the iron foundries and coalfields of Wales, the Midlands and Yorkshire – financed by slavery. The textile industry (Blake's 'Satanic Mills') – financed by slavery.

Elephant herd
The Masai Mara
Kenya
The Slave Route
"No 85"

Thursday 27 December

Elephant herd, the Masai Mara, Kenya

AFRICA

The Africa the Portuguese discovered in the 1400s was predominantly
sophisticated, well governed, tribal, rich and very violent.

Slavery was part of political, economic and social existence.
In some parts, particularly East Africa, it was the basis of lavish and
powerful Empires, exploited by the spread of Islam and the Arabs.

The Europeans (as they did with other commodities) merely traded in slaves.

It was the Africans themselves who provided them, for their own gain.

THE AFRICAN I

THE BANTU TRAGEDY

What has intrigued me for thirty years is trying to understand 'The China Man'. I tried (rather inadequately) to put it on paper in *The Silk Route*. In writing about *The Slave Route*, I am now confronted with a totally new task — understanding 'The African'.

Do you, or can you, understand peoples? Do we not deal with an individual, and, if making a generalisation, commit a wrong?

I think not. I quote from Shiva Naipaul who, with his brother's writings, has so inspired me during years of travel:

'The African persona has come: 'awfully far'

'awfully fast' (a century)

Consequently they are bereft of roots and identity, as are their slave-descendent American and West Indian brothers.

Transition states are full of pain. 'We can lose one's self without gaining another.'

Surely this is the African. Let me explain more closely. Foremost, I am an artist, not a scholar. To an artist, simplicity is the very essence of creating an image. I will approach this problem in a similar vein.

HISTORY

10,000 years ago Hottentots and Bushmen inhabited the African Continent. They were primitive hunter/gatherers both in physical stature and sophistication; but they were the descendants of Homo Sapiens.

Like the Indians of the Americas and the Aborigines of Australasia, they have now become nearly extinct. In the Americas and Australasia the Europeans were the cause. In the African Continent it was the Bantu.

Bantu derives from the word 'Abuntu' meaning people — in thousands of African tribal dialects. 10,000 years ago these Bantu (people) came from 'The Fertile Crescent' (Mesopotamia in the Middle East, and The Levant). Was this the biblical break-up between Cain and Abel? Much of present-day Bantu culture contains traces of Semitic influences from the Arab world.

For the following 10,000 years, these peoples spread into West, Central and East Africa and eventually South — pushing the Bushmen and Hottentots to marginal areas and to extinction.

Essentially pastoral, cattle were central to their societies. Many became highly sophisticated. However, there was one huge problem (not for them, but for the legacy it left).

The Continent was vast. Overgrazing was not a problem. If it occurred, a splinter group could merely move on to proverbial 'pastures new'; establish a new 'group' or tribe. Perhaps it is here that I can understand the African persona.

Herds — the larger the better — meant everything. The ability to expand to ever new pastures eventually resulted in overgrazing and a general destruction of the land (including animals who threatened their herds — primarily lion). I again quote from Shiva Naipaul:

'This perhaps has caused an inadequate grasp of the Laws of Cause and Effect.'

Is this the Bantu tragedy?

THE AFRICAN II

Fossil evidence has revealed (if anything can be believed in life) that humans evolved in Africa and migrated out of this continent some hundred thousand years ago and populated the rest of the world. The first evidence of human existence in the Middle East corresponds to this time.

40,000 years ago man had reached Europe.
35,000 years ago Australasia.
30,000 years ago China.
12,000 years ago the Americas.

10,000 years ago the Bantu people left the Middle East (Mesopotamia) to re-colonise Africa.

Now that the human gene has been 'tapped', we are being told even more detail. If the whole human race is descended from the people who came 'out of Africa', geneticists can now prove that the people who did come 'out of Africa' were descended from ONE African Eve.

DNA, the essential building block of life, is sexual, i.e. it needs a partner DNA with which to combine, making a new and different DNA. Mitochondrial DNA (Mt DNA) is different. It is asexual, i.e. it clones itself. It has remained exactly the same throughout human history. It is only inherited through the female. Male sperm DNA disintegrates after fertilisation.

It appears that every female on earth has the same Mitochondrial DNA. This means that all living females descend from one 'African Eve'. This does not mean that there were not other candidates, but their progeny did not survive.

A sobering thought: we are all literally cousins.

It does add interest to the argument of whether the Old Testament is fact or illustrative fiction. The only problem is ADAM. Eve may well have had a number of partners!

Pelicans, Senegal

THE AFRICAN III

TODAY

Can I search deeper?

There was never a Renaissance in Africa.

Renaissance in Europe meant 'rebirth'. Man became aware of himself and, for the first time, focused on himself – 'the individual'.

It may be argued that the same thing never happened in China. So China, like Africa, is communal. The individual is disposable. The tribe matters.

Suddenly subjecting the Bantu people to move 'awfully far and awfully fast' into an existence of individualism results in a 'dislocation of the Soul'.

A simple example told to me in New Orleans.

A black Afro-American (a middle-class professional), born and bred American, who has never left the United States of America. A white African (a middle-class professional), born and bred African, who has never left Africa.

They meet: it does not matter where.

Total bewilderment on the side of the Afro-American.

Is this not the 'dislocation' of the Bantu Soul?

Flamingos, Senegal, West Africa

Friday 17 March 2000   "No 2"
    Boabab trees   The Dar Al Islam
        at Santiss
    Senegal
        West Africa

H.R.H. *[signature]*

MUNGO MAN

There is a chink in the 'Out of Africa' theory.

In 1974 at Lake Mungo in New South Wales, Australia, ten 60,000 year-old skeletons were discovered — they were anatomically human.

Both DNA and Mitochondrial DNA were analysed. But Mungo Man's Mitochondrial DNA does not exist in modern humans.

If we also go along with Teilhard de Chardin's discovery of Laotian Man in China in 1960, then there is an equal argument for a theory of multi-regional evolution.

Who knows? — Who cares?!!

Baobab tree, Senegal, West Africa

Nairobi, Kenya
CLOWNS
Wednesday 20 December 2000

*N*airobi *is nicknamed 'Nigh Robbery'. It is a perfect example of the present tragic state of Africa.*

I first came to Africa when I was seventeen — to Ethiopia in 1968. I was to work on a cotton plantation owned by the Crown Prince, son of the then Emperor Haile Selassie or, as he was then generally known, 'Highly Suspicious'. Ethiopia was riddled with intrigue at that time.

On the plantation the highland Bantu tribe were 'The Danakil' (in Arabic) or 'The Afar' (in Semitic). They held the plantation workers — 'The Adoimara' — in complete slavery. Torture was normality and at a young age I witnessed my first human executions. Two Adoimara were summarily shot in front of me for being a nuisance.

In an age obsessed with the Western concept of 'rights' this may be difficult to accept. As a sideline, there can be no such thing as a right in existence, not even life itself. Rights may be allied to duties but, amazingly, modern Western society seems not to understand this simple reality.

However, there is something justifiable in hard summary justice.

Haile Selassie's regime may have been harsh, dictatorial and uneasy but the people lived and were fed. The Marxist regime that took over — in the cause of equality — directly caused the death of 4 million people through starvation.

Corruption, greed, incompetence. I could go through a dictionary with one hundred relevant descriptions. Haile Selassie, in contrast, was probably one of Africa's great rulers. Although I never met him I feel an affinity. My uncle was his ADC (aide-de-camp).

Look at the Clowns now:

With limited exceptions one cannot contemplate African heads of state without immediate sensations of outrage and embarrassment.

Amin
Bokassa
Mobutu
Banda
Mugabe

Scores of others who create corruption, genocide and mayhem. Like most things in life, there are flashes of good and sense.

Nyerere
Kaunda

Both enforced the tribal concept of 'lwama': the family.

Tribalism offered security from cradle to grave. Security — this must be fundamental to human existence. This is Godliness as it should be.

Which is perhaps Africa's only hope.

'If the price of goodness is backwardness, then Tanzania will remain backward' (Nyerere).

Where are we going in the West?

Elephant herd, the Masai Mara, Kenya

Wednesday 3 January 2001
Kenya

Vultures
This is Africa — "real" —

Nakuru vultures, Kenya

Nakuru, Kenya
NATURE – THE TRUTH
Sunday 22 December 2001

I witness an astonishing episode.

A zebra is giving calf.

But... disaster. The front legs become caught inside her. The male realises there is a problem. I can do nothing. Nature must take its course. I cannot interfere (the male would kick me to death). I leave.

That night it will either be the hyenas or the vultures that conclude this episode of reality.

The next day I return to the same spot. A kilometre away I see a cloud of vultures. Well over a hundred of these 'grotesque hooded draculas' are in an orgy of a feeding frenzy. They have eaten the calf as well as the insides of the carcass of the zebra. Bloated, they protect the remains of the carcass from other predators, like Roman Legionnaires. They wait, digesting, before continuing another feed. Horrific.

But this is the reality of nature. Not the sentimentality of 'fluffy' sea lions and lion cubs.

Senegal, West Africa
THE HAJ
Friday 17 April 2002

*T*he Haj is the celebration at the end of Ramadan. Central to it is 'The Sacrificial Lamb'. Here it commemorates Abraham's sacrifice of the lamb (instead of Isaac) as opposed to Christianity on Easter Sunday and the 'sacrifice of the Lamb', representing Christ.

Everyone — every man, that is — moves to the town centre and congregates. Row upon row, thousands deep. On their knees, heads to the ground, prostrate, praying towards Mecca.

How many times have I seen this? Each time I still marvel at the devotion — the complete 'surrender' of the human soul to God/Allah. In this one village well over 10,000 people are replicating it.

However, it is still very informal. The children give sugar and salt to the adults as presents in exchange for money — amidst wonderful giggles and smiles.

How much more real than the 'quasi' religious right of 'All Souls' in the West — 'Trick or Treat'? Here, the exchange means something.

The Haj

But then the ugly bit starts. The sacrificing of the lambs. Each family has to produce three lambs. They are in fact far from being lambs. They are large goats, nearly the size of cows.

I am with a family called Mommato — after Mohammed — in their home, in their inner courtyard. Throughout the day the 'Master of Ceremonies' visits each house. In the courtyard three pits have been dug (about the size of an ice bucket), where the animals will be ceremoniously sacrificed. However, this is the most unceremonious sacrifice I have ever witnessed.

The 'Master of Ceremonies' arrives armed with a rather blunt looking kitchen knife. The women and children sit down next to the pit. Meanwhile the three unfortunate sheep are happily munching straw in the corner of the yard — blissfully unaware of their fate.

Sheep number 1: is led very happily and meekly to the first pit, by what I can only describe as four very shiny, hunky, black gents.

Now it turns gruesome. The Master of Ceremonies steps forward. The unfortunate beast is suddenly manhandled and upturned very unceremoniously with his neck over the pit. The Master of Ceremonies, far from 'slitting' the creature's throat, starts 'sawing', whilst the poor thing starts shrieking and struggling. After what appears a dreadfully long passage of time, it expires, blood pouring from its throat into the pit.

Sheep number 2: has continued happily munching straw in the corner. He now stops. He looks to his companion, realizing that something is amiss. Reluctantly, but not struggling (he is not sure), he is led to the second pit. The process is repeated.

Sheep number 3: Has now realized that his odds of further existence are rapidly shortening. He bolts. Our shiny black gent makes a rugger tackle worthy of Twickenham. The creature, bravely fighting, is dragged to the third pit. The process is repeated.

Three sheep expire in succession. Blood reaches the top of the pits in perfect measurement.

What is this extraordinary desire for blood sacrifice that is so engrained in human nature?

We shall come to it, in horrific circumstances, in Central and South America.

Once 'bled' the sheep are hung, head down, on a pole and skinned. The women and children, meanwhile, have happily been watching. Mum, Grandma and assorted aunts and sisters have been 'bashing' sorghum and couscous with long wooden pestles. Those not 'bashing' join the gents in skinning with more knives.

Hygiene is not high on the agenda. Flies and ants join in and the boiling sunshine adds colour to the occasion, which is very jolly.

Finally, in the evening as the sun sets, the extended family sits for a mammoth feast. The testicles are reserved for the patriarchs, grandfather and grandmother. Happiness and smiles. This is religion and the extended family at its best — the corps of their spirituality, the corps of their lives. No fundamentalism, but love and forgiveness.

Oh... how we have lost our way, in the supposedly 'developed' world.

Ouidah, Benin, West Africa
POINT OF NO RETURN
Monday 11 February 2002

*O*uidah, the most notorious of the slaving ports. The Dahomey Kingdom was the most ruthlessly effective of the African slave traders. Five separate forts were built to hold 10,000 slaves at any one time.

The route from the forts to where the slaves were loaded into the ships has become a shrine for Africans and their American brothers — similar to the Via Dolorosa in Jerusalem in emotive terms. This 'Route des Esclaves' is historical fact, whereas the Via Dolorosa is not.

In a rather futile attempt to get a 'feel' for what must have been going through the minds of all those unfortunates, I strip down to my shorts and bare feet and take the route they did.

It is four kilometres from the only surviving fort to the shore where the 'Slavers' (ships) would lie. In the back of the fort, in an open enclosure the size of a tennis court, 2,000 slaves would lie manacled. When the ships arrived the final march would begin — children, females and males chained together.

I leave the enclosure and start out. The route is flat, through what is now savannah, maize and palms. Then it would have been more primary forest. Then, as now, it is a sand track as wide as Sloane Street. Every hundred metres is a Voodoo shrine, commemorating an aspect of tribal ancestry.

The first thing that strikes is the appalling heat and humidity. Walking four kilometres with no clothes and barefoot in this climate is excruciating. At least I am carrying four litres of water. They were not.

The second is the sound. Despite magnificent sandy beaches, West Africa has the Atlantic battling its shores with vast 'breakers'. The thunder of them grows ominously louder as the unfortunates would have approached the shore. They would never have seen the sea before, coming from the northern hinterland.

It takes me two hours and four litres of water to reach the shore. I am utterly shattered but that is irrelevant to what confronts me. The bay is vast. It is exactly as it was then — five miles of golden sand in one huge arc, encircled by palm-fringed jungle. A tourist's dream.

But to the unfortunates it was the last sight of their home — Africa. Can one possibly imagine their feelings as they were loaded on to 'lighters' (small flat-bottomed craft) to be taken through the surf to be lowered into the dark, dank holds of the slaver ships resting at anchor 500 metres beyond the breakers?

That last desperate look at the shore, while listening to the surf, and then into the dark depths of the hold. Horrible.

I suspect I only felt a 'batsqueak' of their anguish.

Gawvé, Benin, West Africa

Thursday 21 Dec
Nakuru
Northern Kenya
" The Slave Route No 81 "

1 large bull,
very lonely
and

LIFE BEFORE EUROPEAN SLAVERY

The vastness of scale: there are 3,000 miles of coastline between Senegal and Angola. Benin (in present-day Nigeria) was the largest city in the early 1500s, bigger than the largest Dutch city of Haarlem. There was an abundance of produce, from cultivated roots and grains to fruits, honey, tobacco — all worked with iron hoes, shovels and axes.

Dress was refined and colourful with natural fibres such as calico and natural dyes such as indigo. The arts flourished (dance, music, painting, and poetry), as did learning and technology (mathematics and astronomy). An especial skill was medicine — in areas that the West has idiotically ignored (because of drug companies).

Luxury goods abounded in bronze, ivory, gold and terracotta. City states were highly sophisticated — such as the Dahomey Kingdom (in present-day Benin), the Ashanti Kingdom (in present-day Ghana) and the Calabar in Nigeria, controlling hundreds of thousands of people.

All this when much of England and Europe was still in the Dark Ages.

Elephants, Masai Mara, Kenya

A shack in Togo, West Africa
BRAINS, TONGUE AND PANCREAS
Saturday 9 February 2002

*T*his has to be the best. As a child in the nursery, my favourite meal was ox tongue with parsley sauce.

I sit in the sweltering heat in Togo at a wooden roadside shack.

In the horrific age of McDonald's, Coca-Cola and fish fingers — and other repulsive frozen things — this is absolute ecstasy.

A dead carcass of a calf is hanging from the roof. Nonchalantly the proprietor of this little shack asks me in perfect Parisian French what I would like. I go for it.

1) Brains (cervelle)
2) Tongue (langue)
3) Sweetbreads (pancreas)

Nonchalantly (a second time) — with knife — the unfortunate animal's tongue is cut out. Its head is sliced open and the brains extracted and from its abdomen the pancreas is plucked out — all done very deftly.

In a large 'wok'-like pan over a charcoal fire they are rapidly sautéed in palm oil, with a handful of assorted herbs — two or three akin to parsley and coriander leaves — and served up with a dash of yoghurt-type cream and chilli in a large wooden bowl, all in under a minute.

The taste — indescribable — sublime.

Escoffier, you were a beginner, or perhaps this Western generation has no idea of how things should taste.

Cape Coast, Ghana

Bab Al Khaora Gate, Tunis

Cotinou, West Africa
APPREHENSION
Thursday 7 February 2002

I get older. I feel fear. I never did. As a soldier in my youth I was immortal. Now at fifty-two it is different.

I am horribly apprehensive when I walk the streets of Cotinou — the slave port of Old Dahomey. I am amidst the most appalling human poverty. Not in the shanty towns of Bombay or the backstreets of Guatemala City have I witnessed what I do here.

But, as you begin to appreciate the people, they have something which I have constantly argued we have now lost in the West. For all the supposed wealth — do I see a smile of happiness on any face in Sloane Square, Fifth Avenue or Hollywood Boulevard?

I begin to know people here. Charming. Apprehension melts away. Complete acceptance from children, despite the fact that you have a white face, which they have never seen before. These are wonderful people, born of love, extended families and tribal organisations.

Love — self help — is the key.

If Africa had been left alone it would still be paradise. Yet around me is chaos.

I walk through the Causeway in Cotinou from sea to lagoon. On both shores there is wasting detritus — one hundred yards width on either side. Three miles long. Three million people live in it. Black plastic is the favoured housing material — cardboard or corrugated iron are not available.

The Marginal Lands, Nefta, Tunisia

And as I write there is a World Summit in South Africa discussing world pollution issues! Something is wrong.

Nefta, The Sahara
DEXTERITY – THE BEAUTY OF THE AFRICAN
Sunday 10 February 2002

Oh! The elegance with which the female African moves. Upright, gliding slowly as if walking on water or ice.

This wondrous, slender creature has (probably) one hundred oranges on a flat basket — arranged as a pyramid, balanced perfectly on her head. One orange falls off. She continues, still with ninety-nine in the pyramid and, without remotely altering her gait, she retrieves the hundredth orange on her foot — kicks it into her left hand and places it with absolute tranquillity back in the basket.

Nefta, The Sahara

Big footballers, like Mr Beckham, are beginners. Another puerile taste of the West may be supermodels. In comparison to this beauty they should not bother to get out of bed — breathtaking…

WEALTH

King Kpengla of Dahomey, trading in 1750, exported over 10,000 slaves – an income of roughly £250,000 in one year.

The biggest estate in England at the time (I won't mention whose) produced around £40,000.

Nefta, The Sahara

Nakuru, Kenya
BUSTARDS AND ANTHRAX
Thursday 19 December 2001

*T*he difference in the local people's concept of diet is wonderful. My host tells me a story of a neighbour, on a nearby ranch — a white settler, post war, Italian.

He sends a hunting party out into the bush to shoot six Greater Bustard birds. (They must not be more than three years old.) These birds are beautiful and, when persuaded to fly (which is difficult), have the most incredible wingspan!

The breasts from these six three-year-olds are then removed, the carcasses discarded. In the pot, they are slowly 'reduced' in order to make a bowl of soup — 'Bustard Consommé'.

This is for one bowl of consommé, but not all is used at once! The next morning: 'Bustard Bullshot'!

What's a Bullshot?
RECIPE
Escoffier never even started!
12 bustard breasts (reduced)
6 parts vodka
3 parts sherry + ice and tabasco

It defies belief! But we have not started!
In the ranch complex the kitchen staff are going to eat something far better. If Bustard Bullshot surprises, let's go for this one:

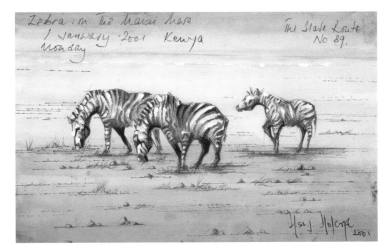

Zebra, Nakuru, Kenya

The local Bantu tribe are the Turkana. A United Nations aid agency vet visited the ranch. He discovered a cow with anthrax and immediately ordered them to bury it in a 20ft deep pit. To them, this was a shameful waste of good meat.

Two days later the Turkana returned and dug it up, appalled that 'good' meat was being wasted. A large feast was had by all!

One person eating 'Greater Bustard Consommé' and drinking 'Bullshot'…while people less than 100m away are eating an anthrax-diseased cow that has been buried in a pit 20ft down for three days.

We are a wonderful species!

Bustard fantastic!

VODUN

Of all human beliefs, the one that continually surfaces around the planet is ancestral worship. All peoples whose lives are dominated by the spiritual, rather than the material, tend towards it in one form or another.

It is central to Vodun (or, as the New World has termed it, 'Voodoo').

Despite Hollywood and the West putting ludicrous, devilish, evil and black twists about it, it is, for me (like so many Eastern concepts), the closest I can come to the ultimate reality or the 'Absolute'.

Vodun's origins are tribal to much of Western African Bantu peoples. A tribal system for 'the whole', rather than the individual, makes it far more natural to accept – for me – than, for example, the Catholic Church, which maintains that Man is created in God's image. This I feel is utter conceit on behalf of Man (unless you have faith – sadly, I don't). It is indicative of the West and the 'I' society which hardly surprisingly has caused an Islamic backlash.

And yet I suppose suicide bombers are somewhat 'I' orientated, although in theory they are doing it for the good of Islam. But all fundamentalism, as Aldous Huxley writing in the 1930s put it, is plain 'goofy'.

Vodun: No. This is belief in goodness and moral good for the benefit of the tribe or group or 'the whole'.

Of course it became distorted by transportation of slaves raised on Vodun to the horrors of Haiti, where it became completely bastardised, although maintaining its power. And power it has.

(I do believe in the power of prayer.)

Dahomey, West Africa
VODUN – SAKPATASIS (VOODOO)
Monday 11 January 2002

'Sakpatasis' is the Fon tribal word for Zombie – bastardised French – but that is what it is still called in both Haiti in the Caribbean and Dahomey, its parent in West Africa.

This is real:

Ancestral worship meant the most enlightened were allowed to live with their forebears to experience afterlife. By various ingredients, snake venom, plant saps etc., a catatonic state could be reached and the body put into catharsis and then buried with the ancestors.

Four or five days later a literal resurrection was performed. Photographic evidence from the 1890s is proof – quite apart from the fact that it is still practised now!

The disturbing bit is that, with the sophisticated practitioners of the art, once resurrection was performed there could be total control of the individual who was resurrected. Hence the 'Zombie' – the living dead.

But absolute fact.

Hippopotami, The river Mara, Kenya

Accra, Ghana

THE GHANAIAN

Saturday 16 February 2002

*T*he Ghanaian: Big – Wonderful – Vivacious. Charming happy people. Life is a ball and they are there to party – and do they! If Africans are full of smiles and goodwill, the Ghanaian is the tops. They rip the white man off, of course.

Wealth to the Ashanti people should naturally be shared, as it always has been – but there is no 'hustling'. When the taxi driver demands ten times the going rate and you say 'bog off' with a smile, he returns with the biggest belly laugh imaginable.

Ghanaian ladies washing

Rhinoceros, Serengeti, Kenya

Give him the correct fare and a generous tip and with a vast array of ivory grinning teeth he is as 'Happy as Larry'.

Although my own faith is now sadly lacking, I believe the Ghanaian's is a legacy of the Baptist and Methodist missionaries – the extraordinary strict moral code of the old-fashioned Swiss and Scottish Presbyterian/Calvinistic Bible punchers. This somehow combines beautifully with the discipline of the extended African family and the duties and loyalty to the tribe. This underlying bedrock to life, wherever I travel, just shines like a beacon throughout the vast majority of humanity, but is so sadly absent in the West.

We have lost something fundamentally essential.

Spirit

Accra, Ghana
HAIRBRUSH
Monday 18 February 2002

I don't believe it. Absurd. Irrational. Funny. But, it happened. Mobile telephones — the desire to get everything smaller and smaller, and look 'designer chic'.

When I travel, I do so with what I call my 'toybox'. A small briefcase and that's it. No luggage.

Amongst my artefacts is a hairbrush. It's a 'nifty little number' — 'designer chic'! It's blue, very small and opens out: it's got a flip-top mirror (which looks like a digital screen): it has twenty bristles with big blobs on the end (which look like buttons you can press).

A charming Ghanaian — a waiter — approaches me offering whatever is available to eat. He looks at my hairbrush, which I have carelessly put on the table.

Western technology has always enthralled the African. He immediately recognises it as a mobile phone!

With a big smile, he picks it up, flips the mirror and starts pushing the bristles, hoping something is going to appear on the crystal screen. Consternation and disappointment when nothing appears!

How embarrassed can you be when you have to explain to a West African that your hairbrush is not a telephone?

Sidi Bin Said — Tunisia

Karoon, Tunisia

2001

Tikal:
Guatemala
Central America

Sketching this
from the top of the
next temple
Suffering from the most
appalling vertigo !!

Tikal, Guatemala

THE AMERICAS

In 1542 Columbus arrived on 'San Salvador', in the present-day Bahamas.

The 'natives' (Indians as Columbus called them, thinking he had reached the Indies)
probably numbered over thirty million.

Unlike Africa before slavery, these societies were as advanced as any in Europe,
the Incas and Aztecs reaching extraordinary heights of sophistication.

But because of three facts — guns, steel and germs —
they were reduced to three million in one hundred years by the Europeans.

Slavery was natural to their societies.
Those not exterminated themselves became enslaved.

THE CARIBBEAN

CUBA

Fascinating. The size of England, it dominates the area. It was, and is, the very key to the Caribbean and the glory of the Spanish Main. Its wealth in terms of natural resources is immense. Rich soil, forest palms and hardwoods, fish resources, not to mention narcotics, make it a mirror image of another naturally rich country: Burma in south-east Asia. Potentially they are two of the richest countries on the planet, but both are two of the poorest. Why?

GREED

Because of their riches, both countries have had histories of the most appalling power struggles. Opposing forces — be they right or left, right or wrong, dictatorial, familial or liberal (always foreign) — have been in conflict since time immemorial. The country and its people are ultimately ruined. This island should economically be a vast beacon of success but no, like Burma, it is locked in a time warp of pitiful poverty because of the power struggles.

And yet I always return to one essential fact.

HAPPINESS

Do I not perceive happiness in so much evidence here? As I did in Burma, Cambodia, Central America, Asia, Africa and most of the Islamic world? How far the West has become lost in its materialistic cocoon. After forty-five years of travelling, reality shouts at you from the streets. Poverty, yes, but as long as there is adequate food to eat, no conflict, disease, or death (i.e. The Four Horses of the Apocalypse) then you have happiness.

And America (where discontent is on most faces) was stunned in September 2001. Walking the 'streets' of the world one could feel that there had to be a major adjustment.

CASTRO'S REGIME

'HISTORY WILL ABSOLVE ME'

This was Castro's 'oeuvre', similar to that of Hitler's *Mein Kampf* or Marx's *Das Kapital*. Castro was a lawyer; consequently the work is pragmatic. However, it tends obviously to the left and, despite talking of freedom, is ultimately suppressive towards the people. It produced a Police State, after the Revolution in 1956, with a very suspicious atmosphere and the accompanying infringement of human rights. A state-controlled economy, as with the rest of the communist world, led to economic stagnation. Today the average take-home pay is only $10 a month.

Yet, unlike the rest of Central and South America, there is no abject poverty. People are protected, with health care and education, the best in Latin America and the Caribbean. (Italians come to Cuba specifically for medical treatment, which is free.) Compare this to other third world countries, where there is not only appalling poverty, but starvation, disease, misery, hopelessness and death.

As a soldier I spent *twenty-two* years training and fighting in conflicts across the planet, involved with counter-insurgency and internal security.

When I look at Cuba and then at the unacceptable side of capitalism, I wonder whether the Revolution was not a good thing. Look at the state of Jamaica, only ten miles way, and the chaos that is in Haiti.

However, somehow the Marxist world-wide model always produces a soulless society. This is the Caribbean. The music and colour are still there, but somehow there is no spirit. Jamaica and Haiti may be poor and chaotic but the people still have soul, spirit, and dignity. Cuba is like the Seychelles in the Indian Ocean — another Marxist regime. Spotlessly clean, no poverty, health and education, total sanitisation, but no Soul.

Today the Establishments, without Soviet support, cannot survive. Castro, pragmatic as ever, has welcomed a tidal wave of tourism and the dollar as a replacement. So the 'time warp' that existed will probably only last another five years and then Cuba will have been absorbed into the amorphous mass of the Coca-Cola culture.

And Castro. Still there. The longest surviving head of state. History, I believe, has absolved him.

I will always turn to Man's spirit, not the material. Give me Madagascar rather than the Seychelles, Haiti rather than Cuba. Yet everywhere I now look, the remaining oasis of man's 'nobility' is slowly being swallowed by capitalism and globalisation.

How strongly I now identify with Islam when not fundamentalist.

Havana
CASTRO: PERSONAL OBSERVATION
Thursday 17 May 2001

All black Africans worship him. Why? Inspiration. I believe he tells, and always has: truth.

He has never been indebted to any 'quasi' international fund (yes, he relied on the Soviet Union), but with the collapse of the Soviet Communist System Cuba went through a similar disastrous crash but, in belief and integrity, chose a communal society — however naïve.

The regime: forty years — where no citizen has paid any tax for those forty years. And their educational and medical facilities put the rest of the world to shame.

The Italians, for example (I perceive the wonderful Roman inheritance), seem to find 'The Best' around the world. Opportunists — yes. Mafia — yes. Yet they come to Cuba for medical treatment. It is 'The Best'. AND IT'S FREE!

Who have their wits about them? NOT THE ENGLISH.

An American Congress decision named 'The Helms Liberation Bill' in 1992 pushed $100 million into Cuba — a lot of money at the time. It was clear that this was designed for dissidence, to unseat Castro.

With the most amazing pragmatism, thirty years after causing a Revolution, against the 'Power' of the American dollar, he has turned to the most obvious vehicle offered to him, by the American dollar... What did he do?

TOURISM!

Havana, Cuba

THE CAPITOL

Monday 14 May 2001

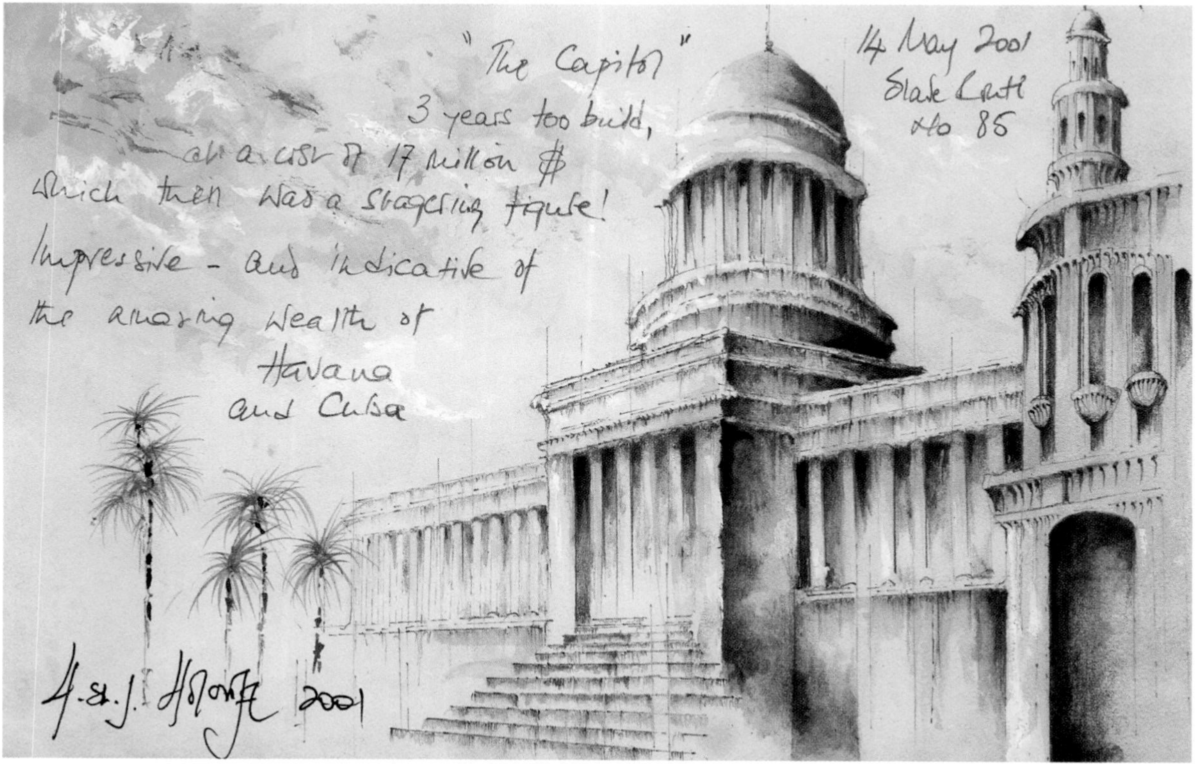
"The Capitol"
3 years too build,
at a cost of 17 million $
which then was a staggering figure!
Impressive - and indicative of
the amazing wealth of
Havana
and Cuba
14 May 2001
Slave Route
No 85
2001

The Capitol, Havana

It appears to have cost $17 million in 1950.

In Castro's time: equivalent to perhaps over $1 billion today. Using 5,000 workers/slaves? It took three years to build.

A replica of The White House in Washington – but bigger and more luxurious, and far more ostentatious.

Impressive: in terms of the wealth this island naturally could have generated. The same as Burma.

What a dreadful waste. Ludicrous largesse created by all totalitarian regimes through ego.

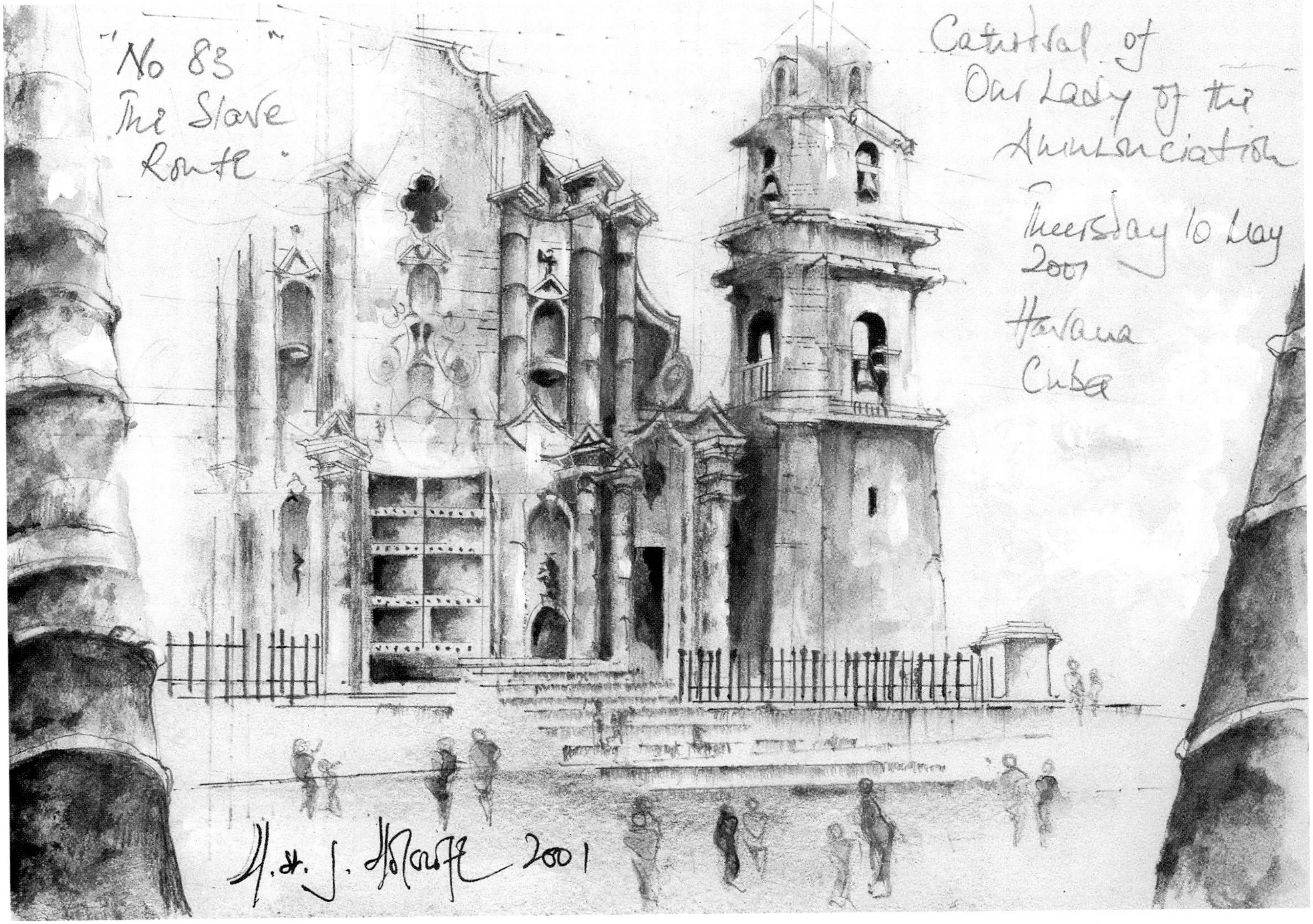
"No 83"
The Slave Route
Cathedral of Our Lady of the Annunciation
Thursday 10 May 2001
Havana
Cuba
2001

Cathedral of Our Lady of the Annunciation, Havana

Havana, Cuba
MUSIC IN CUBA
Saturday 12 May 2001

A *wonderful part of human existence is music. And perhaps I have to say (reluctantly as a painter) that this hits and lifts the soul more than visual stimulation — which makes the life of a painter more precarious that that of a musician. (My mother was a concert pianist and recorded one of the first records.)*

But here in Havana, the music — as in Brazil — is infectious.

Like Brazil, it integrates race. I have not witnessed any race discrimination in the last month (although I know it exists). All are equal.

To sit and listen to the improvisation on a street corner, where the rhythms of descendants of three generations of Spanish and Africans merge, is Magic. The slave trade, however awful, brings with it amazing romance.

The Opera House, Havana, Cuba

Trinidad, Cuba
A WONDERFUL RIP-OFF
Tuesday 15 May 2001

*T*he band and music are good – enthusiastic. (Not brilliant.)

But each tourist bus comes in. Their age, fifty plus. They sit and watch the band play. The leader of the band goes round with:

1. A hat for money: = $
2. CDs for more money: = more $
3. The barman gives everyone a drink: = even more $

After one hour the bus leaves, and they all go out like sheep. Another bus arrives. The process is repeated = awful human gullibility. Ibiza, Torremolinos all over again – the Spanish!

Palacio Revolución, Havana, Cuba

The Market, Havana, Cuba

Santiago, Cuba
MOPPING
Friday 11 May 2001

*I*s this an historical female obsession? It does not matter where I go on the planet, girls are 'mopping'. This is not work – this is desperation!

Boys can build a spaceship, but girls seem to be mopping. Am I on another planet? As a child I remember Spanish maids everywhere, with mops. Everywhere I go in Cuba girls are 'mopping'. What on earth for?

I am sitting in the airport. Lovely ladies mop the floor. Five minutes later more ladies mop – the same floor again and again and again. This is an airport. I wish the same would happen in British National Health hospitals.

Santiago, Cuba
CASTILLO DE SAN PEDRO I
Wednesday 9 May 2001

*T*he name San Pedro always makes me laugh. Pedro keeps cropping up all over the planet. But he was St. Peter 'the rock' or stone, on which the Christian church was to be founded.

The Castillo de San Pedro was founded by Mr Diego de Velázquez, and became Cuba's capital. He then encourages Mr Hernán Cortés to go and be completely vile to everybody in Mexico, wiping out the entire population. 'El Dorado' – the promise of gold was not there.

Havana took over as the central point of Spanish avarice. However, it became the bedrock of all Hispanic revolt, from the earliest days of fighting for independence to present-day Castro. And so it remains one of the most wonderful of America's 'sore thumbs' – right on its doorstep, revolting as much as it can.

It is the heart of the Caribbean. But Santiago in its 'heyday' was such that the King of Spain had a telescope constructed so he could see the city from his palace (in present-day Lisbon).

Castillo de San Pedro

Trinidad, Cuba
SUGAR CANE
Monday 14 May 2001

I am with Sarah, who is happily feeding this parrot with sugar cane. Sarah has always loved animals.

But this is alcoholic sugar cane! After five good munches this parrot falls off his perch – sadly we all do.

HAITI

Port au Prince, Haiti, The Airport
THE CUSTOMS
Wednesday 16 May 2001

T his: beyond Graham Greene's Comedians. *Chaos!*
Sarah (my wife) is not happy. Unwisely I have brought her here.
There is torrential downpour. Wet, and miserable. A gang of Customs officials
resembling the 'Tontons Macoutes' assaults us.

Sarah's cases are attacked. All contents, clothing, female slinky numbers, shoes etc. are
rummaged through.

Then they go for the small bits. Every piece of Sarah's toiletry from lipsticks to creams
are ravaged. She survives. Then they go for me.

I travel with one large briefcase, which is fundamentally my art box. If they thought they
were going to get anywhere with the varying colours of my wife's lipsticks, then watching
them going for my paint tubes was magical.

Cobalt Blue: they were convinced it was opium.

There were now five of these dark-skinned Haitians present. I watch them squeezing
every tube of paint into their mouths. Hysterical!
Who are these baboons? (I cannot describe them as anything else.) The last thing a white
Eurasian is going to do is bring drugs into Haiti. They come out of Haiti!

The highlight was one bespectacled goon who took a big taste of Titanium White — his
face... I creased up!

Who are we? Will the Almighty go back to the drawing board?!

Port au Prince, Haiti
THE OLOFFSON – HAITI'S BIG HOTEL
TAP TAPS
21 May 2001

I am sketching in the hotel garden. There is a deafening sound of drums and blunted music. It gets louder and louder. I look over the wall. There is a vast traffic jam. Tap Taps. A 'Tap Tap' is the most wonderfully coloured transit bus, out of a pantomime.

They are all in gridlock – going nowhere. There must be fifty of them all playing different music. Discothèques on wheels – but totally static. Haiti at its best. Chaos at its best!!

Port au Prince, ,Haiti

Port au Prince, Haiti
THE TRAGEDY
Tuesday 22 May 2001

Sarah came here sixteen years ago for the Carnival. She was delighted.
Now: The President: Aristide – democratically elected? (whatever that means). This country has no history of good guys – except the slave rebel leader Toussaint.

I have witnessed poverty and subjugation in its entirety.

Here, boats docking into the port don't even allow their sailors off as money will go out of whatever corporation is controlling the operation.

This is capitalism at its most grotesque.

Le Cap Haiti, Haiti
THE CITADEL
Sunday 20 May 2001

*T*his has to be one of the most remarkable structures in the world.

It is up there with: *The Pyramids — Egypt*
The Taj Mahal — India
Angkor Wat — Cambodia
K r a c k de Chevalier — Syria
Tikal — Guatemala

However, in many ways it is the 'Best' (not for beauty — St. Peter's, Michelangelo's masterpiece, or the Taj Mahal can take that accolade) — but for its sheer magnificence. 3,000 ft high on a mountain top. 20,000 people built it over five years. Most died. These were not slaves. These were free, after the only successful slave rebellion in the Americas. They were terrified the French would return to reconquer.

And so this massive, gargantuan fortress was constructed with the capability of being self-sufficient and invulnerable. Its only contender is perhaps Masada in present-day Israel.

Haiti

SLAVERY AND AMERICAN INDIANS

Equally as dreadful as the transportation of 20 million Africans to the Americas was the enslavement and subsequent extermination of the native Central American Indians.

Some 15 million died as a result of enslavement and disease brought over by the Spaniards. This was genocide surpassed in history only by Tamerlane in Asia at the same time, and Stalin and Mao Tse Tung in the 20th century.

The Spanish Council for the Indies argued that American Indians, like Africans, could not be classed as humans, having no intelligence and so no soul or free will. As such they were beyond divine consideration. Consequently, Aztecs, Incas, Arawaks, Caribs and the mighty Mayan disappeared, leaving shattered pockets in jungle and mountain. They have survived with their culture, as have pockets of peoples in Africa and Australasia. But the Mayans in Mexico have been the core of successive rebellions against the Spanish oppressor, and a permanent thorn in the dictatorial regimes that are the New World and Mexico.

Trinidad
THE SLAVE TOWER
Sunday 20 May 2001

180ft high. It dominates everything in a 20km radius in every direction, commanding 100 sq.km. All around it are old sugar cane fields, abandoned railways, and distilleries and slave houses. From this vantage point at the top the slave overseer could control the workforce and its operations. I decide to climb it.

I have the most appalling vertigo. (I go dizzy at the top of an escalator!) There are no railings. The steps are wooden slats. There are gaps to the ground between each. As they get higher they get narrower but wider apart. Each level is open to space in all directions.

By level four my legs are jelly.
By level five my stomach joins my legs.
By level six my heart has joined my stomach.
By level seven eyes and head have joined them all.
I am now barely conscious. But the view is incredible.

The journey down allows my anatomy to coalesce again but it takes two hours and a bottle of rum to recover. I presume the 'overseers' didn't have vertigo!

The Slave Tower, Trinidad

Macaws, San Cristobel, Mexico

MACHISMO

One extraordinary outcome of the annihilation of the native population of Central America is the concept of Macho or Machismo. This dominates the behaviour of the whole male population.

But why this extraordinary male arrogance towards women? I think it is because of an underlying psyche.

The ramifications of the Spanish conquest, in terms of the Indians' humiliation, anger and guilt, find their manifestation in the universal condemnation of women. This has gone through generation to generation for five hundred years. The Mayan, were, like many African tribes, warrior peoples. If the males needed someone to blame, somewhere to pinpoint their misfortune, lack of purpose and self-esteem, then the female has become the culprit.

Female subjugation in the rest of the world may occur for religious or economic reasons, but here it is nothing short of male inadequacy. Even if a female is a paragon of virtue she is looked on as a whore and betrayer, and yet it was never the fault of the female. In the remaining fragments of Mayan society the female is today a slave in all but name.

In North America the native Indians today have the highest rate of suicide and drug and alcohol addiction in the United States. A further example similar to the African – 'a dislocation of the Soul'.

San Cristobel, Mexico
GRASSHOPPERS
Friday 25 May 2001

The Mexicans adore them. That is, they eat them!

They appear on a dish in a heap – like 'twiglets', but tasting of turpentine. All their legs fall off in your mouth and you have a sensation of eating burnt toothpicks as well as twiglets and turpentine.

They are everywhere. Squillions of them. They are a tremendous source of nourishment. Either they eat the crops or the humans eat them. A nice ecological balance is maintained.

What surprises me, as I chew through my plateful, is why the French have not got around to eating them as well.

The French, like the Chinese, eat anything and everything. Provence – where I live – is carpeted with these hopping 'canapés' in summer! The French call them cicadas but they appear to me to be exactly the same as in Mexico. I shall try a 'sautéd' plateful when I return perhaps, with some garlic and parsley, and 'flambéd' with Pernod – not turpentine!

Slave Route "
No 101

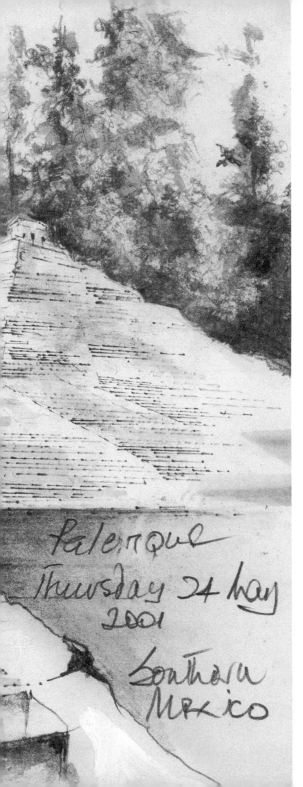

Palenque
Thursday 24 May
2001
Southern
Mexico

Palenque, Mexico

CENTRAL AMERICA

Guatemala
A CATWALK
Wednesday 6 June 2002

I don't know where I am. But I stay in this tiny house in a village that probably has only two hundred people. The Spanish influence is total – dynamic.

We are in the middle of nowhere, and yet the mulatto girls at seven o'clock are dressed as sexily as if they were going down a Milan catwalk. As far as the macho boys are concerned, they are!

Sex drives our lives.

Paris eat your heart out. ...And this is the back of beyond.

San Cristobel, Mexico
A CAFÉ
Wednesday 23 May 2001

I sit with the owner. He is a big, and I mean big, man. Sweat is pouring out of him like a waterfall.

I am here because the food is the best. The owner knows what he is doing. Autocratic to his minions, whom he treats with disdain.

Human nature: wonderful.

I spend a week stumbling through the Mayan ruins, and then return to this café.

He has not moved. He is King. (And still big!) More tortillas and enchiladas keep arriving... This is perfection!

And the sweat keeps pouring.

Toucan, the Pantanel, Brazil

SOUTH AMERICA

BRAZIL

A Mr Pedro Cabral (Pedro again) landed here in 1500: by mistake. He got lost. The Portuguese were doing this all over the world. But, having landed, he built a cross on the beach and called the land 'Terra de Vera Cruz' (Land of the True Cross).

There was little of commercial value in these early days in comparison to Africa and the Far East. The only thing of any interest was what the Indians called 'pau brazil' (Brazil wood). This, which produces a distinctive red dye, was the only commercial commodity and gave Brazil its modern-day name.

EXTERMINATION OF THE INDIANS

It was not war. Although that was a major contribution.

The Europeans introduced germs, from which the indigenous peoples had no immune protection.

Influenza, dysentery, malaria, smallpox – all came from Europe. This was the same as the 'Black Death' in Europe coming from Central Asia. This was not decimation (i.e. death of one in ten) but an annihilation of the population.

Impanema Beach, Rio de Janeiro, Brazil
BRAZILIAN ELECTION DAY
Saturday 5 October 2002

O*n the beach: normally a haze of fog, sea, mist and sometimes sunshine. Saturday. Today there is a mist of marijuana smoke.*

Passive smoking? You are as high as a kite just breathing in the atmosphere.

The beach is heavily policed. These police have eyes the size of pinheads! What are they on?

The human species never ceases to amaze me.

Control? This is Election Day. There was extraordinary activity downtown yesterday in the supermarkets. The reason? On Election Day the selling of alcohol is banned throughout Brazil, from the supermarkets to the Sheraton Hotel.

The Brazilians went into a feeding frenzy of stocking up hooch for the day. Only 30% managed to stagger to vote.

Who won? Who cares? Stay on the beach.

And yet the shanty towns of São Paolo equal, if not outdo, the worst of Bombay or West Africa. And this was the country hailed by economic professors at Oxford and Cambridge in the late '60s as being the next Superpower – what happened?

Iguaco Falls, Paraguay
WATERCOLOUR IN THE RAIN
Wednesday 30 May 2001

It is bucketing down water.

Going into the jungle in the rainy season is not a good idea. The rain comes down so fast; it seems to boil on the floor. I am attempting a watercolour of the falls. Watercolour does not really work in a torrential downpour!

It ended up with a somewhat impressionistic effect.

But — always remember — the Impressionists painted the way they did because they were half blind. Monet could not see a thing.

So perhaps mine are not so bad!

Iguaco Falls, Paraguay

The Pantanel, Brazil
MACAWS
Wednesday 26 May 2001

*T*hey are amazing.

Quite apart from their extraordinary shocking and outrageous colours, they're the noisiest creatures I have heard. Worse than monkeys. What are they saying to each other? Only Heaven knows. Worse than women.

But to see them in clusters within the jungle is inspiring. They are in perpetual movement. Arguing, canoodling, grooming, chattering. It's like a vast cocktail party.

I have tried to sketch them in the jungle. You cannot. They are too quick and too high. So you do it when they are caged in a hotel or zoo.

And the most extraordinary thing is that they know — in some way — what you are doing. Their very naturalness (the arguing, canoodling, and grooming) — fades.

They pose — like actresses or supermodels.

Sad.

Macaws, the Pantanel, Brazil

Rio de Janeiro, Brazil
THE BRAZILIAN
5 October 2002

He is the Ghanaian of South America. Although most slaves transported to Brazil came from Angola, many came from present-day Ghana. Just like the Ghanaian, life is for living, and their zest for it is impressive. But as in Los Angeles they have become obsessed with the body beautiful. Which I find a little tedious.

None the less, they live life to the full. And do they drink?! They put the French and me to shame. 'Cachaca' (sugar cane rum) goes down gullets by the gallon! And it blows your head off.

THE SWORD, THE CROSS, AND THE INDIANS

The history was one of cruelty, piracy, arson, enslavement and a total disregard for the prevailing social and religious customs of the Indians. The Church/the Cross were heavily instigated.

Many of the churches owned sugar plantations and so were implicitly involved – the Dominicans and Jesuits in particular.

But all was not bad. There were many 'Brotherhoods' with great spiritual intent: from the likes of Francis Xavier to the 'Brotherhood of Our Lady, Mother of God, Virgin Mary of Mercy' – commonly know as the 'Misericordia'.

Great good accompanied appalling bad, as it still does today.

SUGAR

An invention of Brazil. It is not a complicated crop. With fertile land and good irrigation the sugar cane grows like a weed.

Introduce it to Europe, or turn it into rum, with the slaves to harvest it.

Whammy!

Hummingbird and orchid, the Pantanel, Brazil

Brasilia, Brazil
ANOTHER MEAL
Friday 16 October 2002

*I*t started with:

1. *'Farofa de Abobora'* – this is pumpkin (passable)
Next came:
2. *'Feigao de corda'* – beans (well, a bean is a bean)
Next came:
3. *'Cabrito com Piarao e Brocolis'* (This was goat. The broccoli bit I could recognise. The piarao was some sort of tapioca which reminded me of prep school lunches)
I gave up after that!

How is it that wherever the Portuguese go they manage to make one of life's pleasures excruciating torture?

(Incidentally, I lost nearly two stone after six weeks in Brazil!)

Hummingbirds and ginger flowers,
the Pantanel, Brazil

MINAS GERAIS

Minas Gerais means the 'General Area of Mines'. The mines are centred on a mountain chain 12km long. The chain contains the most concentrated veins of gold and gemstones in the world.

At the height of production in the 1700s the area was producing 80% of the world's gold.

Oro Puerto means 'Black Gold'. The veins are within graphite, which produces soft black rock. The gold veins produce only gold dust, not nuggets. Hence 'Black Gold' – which had to be 'pan' sifted.

Oro Puerto, Minas Gerais, Brazil
THE SLAVES
Wednesday 16 October 2002

*F*ascinating. *The extent to which the Portuguese exploited both mountain and slaves. This was slavery at its worst – worse than the French in Haiti – and that is saying something. As an example, let's take an imaginary slave from Angola:*

Having been taken by a neighbouring tribe in conflict – shackled with his kin – it could have been a forced march to the sea, taking six months. Possibly one quarter may have died on this leg of the journey. On the Middle Passage, taking three months, another quarter of them might die.

On arriving in Bahia (Salvador) it took another six months' forced march to reach Minas Gerais – during which another quarter might die.

The mathematics are stark. Out of one hundred slaves leaving Angola only twenty-five to thirty would actually reach Minas Gerais.

Oro Puerto, Minas Gerais, Brazil

Oro Puerto, Minas Gerais, Oro Puerto
DOWN A MINE
Wednesday 16 October 2002

I have a miner's helmet, boots, lamp and black guide called Pedro! He is invisible in the dark!

We go down a shaft.

It is estimated that there are two to three thousand shafts. They tunnel into the mountain. The width of a man and the height of a man. Probably 1,000 kilometres of them. Hacked out by slaves.

Production of gold or gemstones was hit and miss. It could take two years of tunnelling producing nothing but shale and graphite before a gold vein was struck. By then thousands of slaves would have died in the most pitiable of conditions. Half a million slaves worked these mines. The shafts were made with hammer and chisel through solid rock, shale and limestone. Light was provided by burning sulphur. Having entered the mountain the slaves never left, sleeping where they hacked and shackled to their comrades. With the dust and sulphur their lungs collapsed.

The longest they survived was three years – most only six months. Knowing only the dark and the manioc they were fed to sustain them.

My guide lopes ahead. I bang my head, stub my toes, and fall on my face. The black graphite is like black molasses and smells revolting. You are covered in gunk within five minutes. We go miles (probably only 100 yards) – but it takes hours. It is awful. It is like being on the end of a 'dip stick'.

I grovel about for four hours. Sometimes in pitch blackness, as Pedro disappears regularly. I have no concept of time or space. I am drowning, surrounded by quartz, shale, graphite, pyrite, topaz, aquamarine, tourmaline, citrine and emerald. Awful. Snow White's Seven Dwarfs should all have been grumpy! I vow never to buy Sarah any jewellery again as I 'slop about' in this black porridge.

Minas Gerais represents the most sordid of past slavery. This was human life made incomprehensibly awful, and it then ended in three years – and what for?

The want of riches. For females in Europe to have baubles around their necks, wrists and fingers. For the clergy to decorate their churches.

This is not political correctness.

It is a testimony of Man's inhumanity to Man, out of greed and vanity. And the Portuguese? I am reluctant to say – in the forefront.

The legacy of Brazil is curious. Because of inter-breeding over five hundred years there is not the same racial tension as in North America and Europe. But economically it is still a very divided society.

THE ENGLISH CONNECTION

The gold from graphite is powder. Consequently the most extraordinary trading connection started.

By the 1700s England was beginning the Industrial Revolution. One of the offshoots of 'modern' manufacturing at the time was the technology to produce gold leaf. No one but the English had this technique.

Gold from Oro Puerto was shipped to Portugal, taxed, and then shipped to England to be transformed into gold leaf. This was then shipped back to Brazil. Hence the glittering rococo interiors of South American Portuguese churches.

Portugal became one of Britain's greatest allies in terms of mutual benefit and we have been suffering from gout as a result of port ever since!

Bahia (Salvador), Brazil
CHRIST CRUCIFIED – 'PIETÀ'
Wednesday 6 November 2002

This ranks with Michelangelo. Here is the epitome of human suffering. Yet beauty and the sublime hit you like a hammer.

The poised composition in carved cedarwood is breathtaking. The colouring startling. Dark putrefied wounds blackened by banana skins. Blood drops of 2,500 rubies are intertwined within the black wounds.

A black slave who was the property of the Carmelite order in Salvador, Bahia, carved this.

He is up there with Tintoretto's crucifixion in the Scuola San Rocco in Venice as with — for me — Michelangelo's 'Bacchus' in the Uffizi Museum in Florence.

It restores what little faith I have in humanity. And this is the work of an African slave. Don't talk to me about racial inequality. We all come out of Africa.

Bahia, Brazil
I AM NAÏVE
Tuesday 5 November 2002

The Knights Templar. The Masonic Lodge. Could I have imagined that the Masons (the Knights Templar) were behind the Slave Trade, the Spanish Inquisition and the havoc in Palestine during the Crusades?

The evidence is here in Salvador. There are several Jesuit and Franciscan churches, Masonic in their design. These were Catholic churches, but their rituals were not Catholic. Separate floors in the church practised different concepts. An extraordinary diversity of hybrid religions developed — Voodoo, Christian and Masonic practices.

Despite this religious melting pot and chaos, looking at the architecture and decorations of the churches you feel the exuberance of faith. Whatever their beliefs, it still makes your spirit soar. It gives credence to something higher than material man.

Oro Puerto, Minas Gerais, Brazil
SLAVERY AT ITS WORST
Wednesday 16 October 2002

*I*ndicative of the brutality of the Portuguese is a sculpture in one of the churches in Oro Puerto, called 'Our Lady of Pila'.

This sculpture is of the Archangel Gabriel who appeared and announced to the Virgin Mary the forthcoming birth of her child

Jesu Christus – 'The Anointed One'. It is gold.

The Archangel Gabriel is, throughout Christianity, depicted as the destroyer of Satan or the serpent, speared by him at his feet. Good over Evil.

This dreadful icon has the Archangel spearing a black slave in graphic detail ... at his feet – instead of the Devil. The Portuguese believed the Africans were soulless animals.

Ibis nesting, the Pantanel, Brazil

THE AMAZON

This is one BIG river (the river Yangtze in China is a peanut in comparison). The Amazon is 6,200 miles long. A basin of six million square miles — a quarter of the world's fresh water.

Halfway down at Manaus (3,000 miles from the sea) it is four miles wide. It has over 1,000 tributaries. It pushes more water into the Atlantic in twenty-four hours than the Thames does into the Channel in a year. 100 miles into the Atlantic the water is still fresh.

For all the environmental 'argy-bargy' the Amazon, compared with the rest of the planet, is untouched. Perhaps 10% may have been deforested — and this is probably happening at an alarming rate — but there is a mind-boggling amount still out there. Compare this with Africa!

RAINFOREST

Awe-inspiring. Tropical rainforest has an aura of still and unfathomable power — gargantuan, massive, a huge living thing.

Once inside the forest, perceptions of distance are hard to maintain. Hence the fascination with trying to capture it on canvas.

It disorientates. You are lost, but not only in the physical sense. The absolute self-sufficiency of the forest confuses the human sense of purpose and self-esteem. You are inadequate — futile. The same feeling I have had on the edge of a volcano.

It tests your faith in anything.

THE SATALÉ

It does not make very much difference which country you are in when on the upper reaches of the Amazon.

I am spending a week with the Satalé. This is a tribe — or, more precisely, an extended family. They live in movable palm dwellings and are wonderfully happy.

But then they have adapted to the jungle in a way I have not.

Jungle, the Amazon

Paraguay — Bolivia — Brazil?!
DINNER WITH THE SATALÉ
Friday 11 October 2002

I thought I had eaten almost everything: *monkey brains in China, rats in Ethiopia, pig's head in Spain, sheep's testicles in Syria, locusts in Mexico, roast cow at Claridges, London — but this meal is the best.*

First course: baby coconut. Especially interesting as a huge great lava bug has grown inside it. This is the particular delicacy of the tribe. It is white and wobbly and the size of a golf ball. Down it goes. It is like eating a huge squelchy baked bean with a somewhat peppery flavour — delicious. (I left the coconut.)

Second course: a bowl full of red ants. Now these are really good. They catch them on a stick using palm sap. Attracted by the sap all the ants end up stuck on the stick. They are really very good, crunchy with a sort of lemony flavour with, again, a slight peppery taste. They don't have to be cooked, no preparation, just eaten in handfuls. The children adore them. Scrummy!

Marco Pierre White, you have not started! Despite the fact that at my fiftieth birthday party your cooking was brilliant.

Ibis in flight, the Upper Amazon

The Upper Amazon, Bolivia?
INITIATION
Saturday 10 October 2002

I thought circumcision ceremonies in Africa were a little extreme. Try this South American one.

The young would-be adult is tied to a tree. A large palm leaf is filled with a particular species of black ants. These are an inch long and have a poisonous bite. The leaf is then wrapped around his marital equipment. The ants have a ball ... metaphorically speaking. The boy grits his teeth and says 'Wow'. These things really hurt.

It is not the 'macho' side which is significant.

It has now been proved by modern science (as if the Indians had not discovered this thousands of years ago) that the ant stings:

1. Inoculate and are an antidote to mosquito bites, malaria, yellow fever and some snake bites and enhance the natural immune system.

2. Have an aphrodisiac effect. More important to tribal survival is his reaction to a few hundred ants on him, as he springs into life putting Errol Flynn to shame. Viagra is a beginner.

Modern Western girl — eat your heart out!

The Pantanel, Bolivia or Paraguay?
BLISS
Friday 25 October 2002

I am on a wooden veranda. A hut. Above a flat calm lake covered with lily pads. This is the back of beyond. I am surrounded by these awful macaws. They make a noise — like most females. They are beautiful — like most females.

The sun is four times the size of the one in Provence and I am contentedly being baked alive.

It is eight o'clock in the morning! I have never been through such heat. There are wonderful occasions when I feel so remote from the human race. Sublime.

The macaws and me. Next day — Carumba. You bet!

Within the image (handwritten notes):

Sunday 6 October 2002
/Ganço: Brazil

Slave Route
No. 350

Macaws.
The Most Disagreeable
of Birds:-
Because of
their beuty
and
subsequent

Carumba, Bolivia
CARUMBA
Saturday 27 October 2002

*A*round 1500 the Portuguese arrived in this area and there were probably six million indigenous Indians. Three main tribes predominated: Guarani, Tupi, Tupna (all hybrid Spanish translations).

There were actually 1,000 different tribes. This was the world of Rousseau and Defoe: 'The Noble Savage', 'Living in Paradise'. The fact that they were enslaving, sacrificing and eating each other is a minor irrelevance.

Were they noble? I expect just hungry!

Macaws, the Amazon

Caiman – South American alligators

The Pantanal, Bolivia, Upper Amazon
PIRANHA
Friday 11 October 2002

*T*he Satalé take me fishing.

Piranha is their staple diet, eaten with manioc root.

Piranha are delicious. They are only about three inches long, and taste somewhat like skate. Being very pompous and rather stupid, I felt the need to know how a piranha works.

I put my hand in the water – actually, one finger, the middle finger of the left hand. Instantly a piranha strikes. This fish works at the speed of light. I instinctively pull my finger out of the water. The piranha is still clinging on. I watch it eat up the flesh along the length of the finger in a circular motion. Dentists in the West with electric drill do not compare.

He hangs on as though his life depended on it. Well of course it does!

Who invented these things? Was God really thinking rationally? He should go back to the drawing board again.

I eat the bastard for supper that night! Who eats who on this planet?

Bolivia, South America
CAIMAN
Saturday 26 October 2002

In a canoe with Benito. He is rather good-looking. We are on the edge of a lake. With sign language I make him stop on the water's edge. The stillness is astonishing. Cranes and storks walk through the shallows causing a mere ripple in the waters.

It is sunset. All is turning a wonderful shade of violet. No wind. The water is flat. This is tranquillity to soothe the most hardened of hearts. I sketch. Fine. Until a caiman (alligator) climbs into the canoe from the bank!

How life can change in an instant. I am thinking the world is paradise, then this thing is about to eat me.

Benito is one end of the canoe, I at the other. This monster crawls up the canoe. He is aiming for my right leg. I can see it in his eyes.

This thing is only 4ft long. But its mouth and teeth are 3ft long. It moves in slow motion. This is nightmare. When they strike it's quick!

Now I am facing this thing as it comes up the canoe. I was a soldier for twenty-two years, but now my only weapon is a pencil, a paint-brush and a yellow plastic paddle — (from Woolworth's?) Something ideal for your baby daughters in a theme park — not something you feel confident with when you are about to be eaten on the Amazon.

My knee jerk reaction is to leg it into the water, but as I have described I have already lost a finger to a piranha.

We are often faced with hard decisions in life.

This one: Take a gamble with the piranha
Take a gamble with the caiman

This is like the Devil or the deep blue sea.

Time is moving fast. Micro seconds. I decide to go for the caiman with the plastic paddle, as opposed to the pencil or paintbrush. From my years as a soldier I have learnt one basic rule: the best form of defence is attack.

My leg is at stake (steak?, literally). This is survival.

With plastic paddle in hand, and adrenalin pumping through me, I thump the caiman on its snout with all the force I can muster. Never has this caiman been hit with a plastic yellow paddle by a mad Englishman. It is, luckily, more terrified and shocked than I am, and shoots off the canoe as though it had met Armageddon.

I collapse. Benito washes my head with water and I come down to earth again. I reflect.

I suddenly have great sympathy with the animal. If you are a caiman going about your business in the waters of the upper reaches of the Amazon, eating what you can, then how awful to meet a madman with a plastic yellow paddle.

Hummingbird and orchid

CONCLUSION

ABOLITION

There had always been objections to the Atlantic slave trade throughout history. However, they rarely came to anything because 'double standards' were involved, as all those in power were directly, or indirectly, financially involved in the trade.

The real abolition movement started in North America with the Baptists in Carolina and the Presbyterians in Pennsylvania. The first example was the condemning of the 'Witches of Salem'. They were in fact all slave traders.

The Quakers of Newport, Massachusetts and Rhode Island, all of whom were large slave owners, also began to realise the incompatibility of slavery with Christian principles.

But there was another reason in North America beyond philanthropy, and that was the fear of rebellion. There was instant pressure to reduce the number of slaves coming in because of this.

This was the period of the Enlightenment – the great wave of ideas and emotions of which Voltaire was the grand figure. He wrote in 1764:

'People who traffic in their own children are more condemnable than the buyer.' – condemning both the Africans and the slavers.

Together with the American beginnings, the movement finally took off in the Atlantic.

AN EVOCATION OF THE SLAVE TRADE

One of the first Englishmen openly to condemn slavery was James Thomson. In 1726 he was writing about the horrors of the Middle Passage, describing a shark following a slave ship:

'Lured by the scent of rank disease and death – behold – he, rushing, cuts the briny flood, as swiftly as the gale will bear the ship along. And from the partners of this cruel trade, which spoils unhappy Guinea of her sons, demands his share of the prey'.

This reflection gains poignancy if it is recalled that James Thomson was the author of the most patriotic verse in English:

'Rule, Britannia'
'Britons never will be slaves'

And the British were the biggest of the slave traders.

Macaws, the Amazon

86 The Slave Route

NUMBERS

How can we possibly know? 20 million is the accepted figure – from Africa to the Americas.

But the 'Dickensian' type of trade documentation is probably way off the mark. And that documentation is only from the English. The reality, I think, is much wider. Think for example of:

Pirating
Silent partners
All forms of corruption and tax evasion

None can be analysed. The nations involved:

Portugal
Spain
France
Holland
England

And this is only to the Americas.

Whatever the real numbers, the lasting legacy is one of 'trauma and dislocation' —
to the Bantu peoples of Africa and the native Indians of the Americas.
The enormity of this, on both sides of the Atlantic, can never be analysed.
I suspect it is a major factor in explaining the chaos that is Africa today,
and the instability that is characteristic of much of Central and South America.
A sad culmination of Man's incessant quest for wealth.